Published simultaneously in 1995 by Exley Publications in Great Britain, and Exley Giftbooks in the USA.

Selection and arrangement © Helen Exley 1995
The moral right of the author has been asserted.
ISBN 1-85015-622-0

Edited by Helen Exley.
Picture research by Image Select International.
Typeset by Delta, Watford.
Printed in China.

12 11 10 9 8 7 6 5 4

Exley Publications Ltd, 16 Chalk Hill, Watford, Herts WD1 4BN, UK.
Exley Giftbooks, 232 Madison Avenue, Suite 1206, New York, USA.

Exley Publications gratefully acknowledges permission to reproduce copyright material. Whilst every effort has been made to trace copyright holders and acknowledge sources and artists, the publishers would be pleased to hear from any not here acknowledged. NIKKI GIOVANNI: extract from *A Poem Of Friendship* from *"Cotton Candy On A Rainy Day"* © 1978 Nikki Giovanni. By permission of William Morrow and Co. Inc.; C. S. LEWIS: extracts from *The Four Loves: Friendship* published by Fount, a division of HarperCollins Publishers Ltd., © C.S. Lewis Pte. Ltd. 1960; TARA McKENZIE: extracts from *Cosmopolitan* magazine, April 1995; EUDORA WELTY: extract from *"The Norton Book Of Friendship"* published by W. W. Norton & Co.Ltd., 1991.
Picture credits: Exley Publications is very grateful to the following individuals and organizations for permission to reproduce their pictures: Alinari (AL), Archiv für Kunst (AKG), Bridgeman Art Library (BAL), Chris Beetles Gallery (CBG), Christie's Colour Library (CCL), Edimedia (EDM), Fine Art Photographic Library (FAP), Scala (SCA). Cover: Peter Severin Kroyer (BAL); title page: John Finnie (EDM); page 6: © 1995 Ruggero Focardi (SCA); page 9: © 1995 "Schools Out", Allan Rohan Crite, National Museum of American Art (BAL); page 10: Plinio Nomellini (AL); page 12/13: Tadeusz Makowski (AKG); page 15: © 1995 Georges Van Zeuenbergen (BAL); page 16: Nikolai Petrovich Bogdanov-Bel'skii (EDM); page 18: © 1995 Luis Graner Arrufi (BAL); page 20: © 1995 Erik Werenskiold (BAL); page 23: Silvestro Lega (SCA); page 24: © 1995 John Singer Sargent (EDM); page 26: © 1995 Frederick Clement (EDM); page 28: Gillray (BAL); page 30: Alexander M. Rossi (EDM); page 33: Carl Christian Carlsen (BAL); page 34: © 1995 Henry Jules Jean Geoffroy (EDM); page 37: © 1995 Harold Harvey (BAL); page 39: © 1995 Wilfried Falkenthal (AKG); page 40: © 1995 Lucy Willis (CBG); page 43: Silvestro Lega (SCA); page 45: Thomas Liddall Armitage (FAP); page 46: Franz von Lenbach (AKG); page 49: © 1995 C.C. Hornung Jensen (CCL); page 51: Peter Severin Kroyer (BAL); page 53: © 1995 Edgar Klier (AKG); page 54: Konstantin Korowin (AKG); page 57: Theodore Gerard (FAP); page 59: Charles Hodge Mackie (BAL); page 61: Giovanni Fattori (SCA).

FRIENDSHIP

THE BEST QUOTES AND THE MOST BEAUTIFUL PICTURES

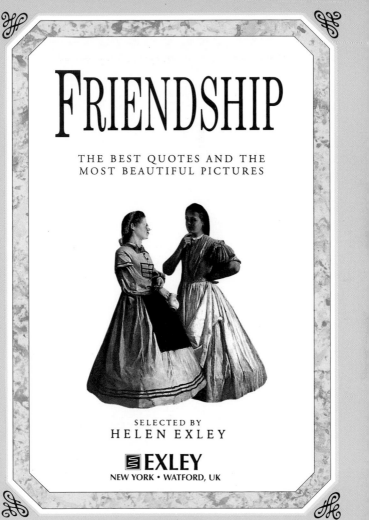

SELECTED BY
HELEN EXLEY

≣EXLEY
NEW YORK • WATFORD, UK

OF ALL HAPPINESSES…

Of all happinesses, the most charming is
that of a firm and gentle friendship. It
sweetens all our cares, dispels our
sorrows, and counsels us in all
extremities.

SENECA (4B.C.-A.D.65)

The very society of joy redoubles it; so
that, while it lights upon my friend it
rebounds upon myself, and the brighter
his candle burns the more easily will
it light mine.

ROBERT SOUTH (1634-1716)

$\mathcal{I}$t is a good thing to be rich, and a good thing to be strong, but it is a better thing to be loved of many friends.

EURIPIDES (C.485-406 B.C.)

What is more indefatigable in toil, when there is occasion for toil, than a friend? Who is readier to rejoice in one's good fortune? Whose praise is sweeter? From whose lips does one learn the truth with less pain? What fortress, what bulwarks, what arms are more steadfast than loyal hearts?

SAINT JOHN CHRYSOSTOM (C.345-407), FROM "FIRST DISCOURSE ON KINGSHIP"

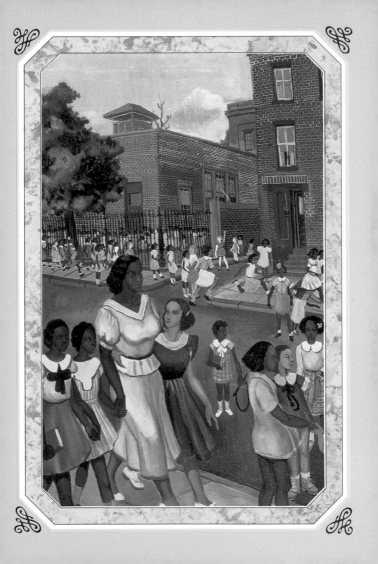

*T*here is no shop anywhere where one can buy friendship....

ANTOINE DE SAINT-EXUPERY (1900-1944)
FROM "*THE LITTLE PRINCE*"

*A poor man may be said to be rich in the
midst of his poverty, so long as he enjoys the
interior sunshine of a devoted friend. The
wealthiest of men, on the contrary,
is poor and miserable, if he has no
friend to whom he can disclose the
secrets of his heart.*

JAMES GIBBONS (1834-1921)

So long as we love we serve; so long as we are loved by others, I would almost say that we are indispensable; and no man is useless while he has a friend.

ROBERT LOUIS STEVENSON (1850-1894)

Friendship hath the skill and observance of the best physician; the diligence and vigilance of the best nurse; and the tenderness and patience of the best mother.

LORD CLARENDON

On the outskirts of Havana, they call friends *mi tierra,* my country, or *mi sangre,* my blood.
In Caracas, a friend is *mi pana,* my bread, or *mi llave,* my key.

EDUARDO GALEANO, b.1940,
FROM *"THE BOOK OF EMBRACES"*

Friendship, a dear balm –
Whose coming is as light and music are
'Mid dissonance and gloom: – a star
Which moves not 'mid the moving
heavens alone:
A smile among dark frowns :
a beloved light:
A solitude, a refuge, a delight.

PERCY BYSSHE SHELLEY (1792-1822)

FREE TO BE OURSELVES

When we come into contact with our friend we enter into a different environment where the air we breathe is more pure, the sounds we hear are sharper, the colors we see more dramatic, and the ideas we think quicker and more insightful. The physical environment is completely different, because now we are in a situation not only where we are free to be ourselves but where we have no choice.

ANDREW M. GREELEY, b.1928,
FROM "THE FRIENDSHIP GAME"

SOMEONE TO SHARE

$\mathcal{I}$ want someone to laugh with me,
someone to be grave with me, someone
to please me and help my discrimination
with his or her own remark, and at times,
no doubt, to admire my acuteness and
penetration.

ROBERT BURNS (1759-1796)

We read more deeply, remember more clearly, enjoy events with greater pleasure if we have a friend to share with.

PAM BROWN, b.1928

I with you, and you with me,
Miles are short with company.

GEORGE ELIOT (MARY ANN EVANS)
(1819-1880)

Let the soul be assured that somewhere in the universe it should rejoin its friend, and it would be content and cheerful alone for a thousand years.

RALPH WALDO EMERSON (1803-1882),
FROM "ESSAYS: FRIENDSHIP"

I wish that friendship should have feet, as well as eyes and eloquence. It must plant itself on the ground, before it walks over the moon.

RALPH WALDO EMERSON (1803-1882), FROM "ESSAYS: FRIENDSHIP"

When friendship once is rooted fast
It is plant no storm can blast.

FROM A 19TH CENTURY CALLING CARD

Do not let your vanity and self-love make you suppose that people become your friends at first sight, or even upon a short acquaintance. Real friendship is a slow grower.

LORD CHESTERFIELD ((1694-1773)

$\mathcal{I}$t is when two such [kindred souls] discover one another … that Friendship is born. And instantly they stand together in an immense solitude.

C.S. LEWIS (1898-1963),
FROM "*THE FOUR LOVES: FRIENDSHIP*"

Friendship is a strong and habitual inclination in two persons to promote the good and happiness of one another.

EUSTACE BUDGELL (1686-1737)

Love and friendship are the discoveries of ourselves in others, and our delight in the recognition….

ALEXANDER SMITH (1830-1867)

What is a friend? A single soul dwelling in two bodies.

ARISTOTLE (384-322 B.C.)

SOMEONE WHO CARES

… many of us are more dependent than at any other time in history upon friendships that truly work for us, bring us joy and give us a sense of well-being and belonging. We need someone who cares when we're sick or upset or have good news to share.

ADELAIDE BRY

Friendship is the poor relation of Man's animal urges; and like poor relations, it stands by us when food, drink, sex and money have blown on another guy's dice. Friendship, like home, is where we go when nobody else will have us.

JULIE BURCHILL
FROM "THE SUNDAY TIMES",
FEBRUARY 12, 1995

[Friendship is] a general and universal fire, but temperate and equal, a constant established heat, all gentle and smooth, without poignancy or roughness.

MICHEL EYQUEM DE MONTAIGNE
(1533-1592), FROM *"OF FRIENDSHIP"*

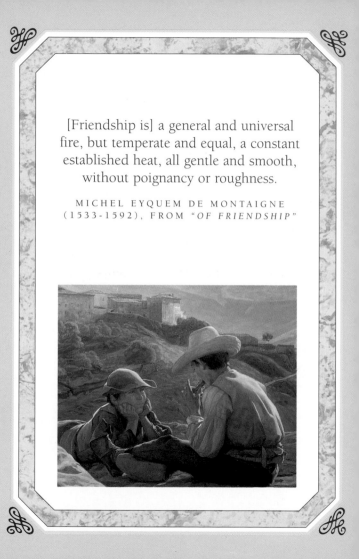

A friend that you have to buy won't be worth what you pay for him, no matter what that may be.

GEORGE D. PRENTICE,
FROM *"PRENTICEANA"*

I hate the prostitution of the name of friendship to signify modish and worldly alliances. I much prefer the company of plough-boys and tin-pedlars to the silken and perfumed amity which only celebrates its days of encounter by a frivolous display, by rides in a curricle, and dinners at the best taverns.

RALPH WALDO EMERSON (1803-1882),
FROM *"ESSAYS: FRIENDSHIP"*

$\mathcal{I}$t is one of the blessings of old friends that you can afford to be stupid with them.

RALPH WALDO EMERSON (1803-1882)

If you want to know who your friends are, lie by the roadside and pretend to be drunk.

JAMAICAN SAYING

$\mathcal{A}$ friend is someone who knows all about you and loves you just the same.

ANONYMOUS

To find a friend one must close one eye. To keep him – two!

NORMAN DOUGLAS (1868-1952)

A friend never tells you to "pull yourself together".

PAM BROWN, b.1928

When my friends are one-eyed, I look at them in profile.

JOSEPH JOUBERT (1754-1824)

ON NEUTRAL GROUND

THAT IS THE KINGLINESS OF FRIENDSHIP.
WE MEET LIKE SOVEREIGN PRINCES OF
INDEPENDENT STATES, ABROAD, ON NEUTRAL
GROUND, FREED FROM OUR CONTEXTS. THIS
LOVE (ESSENTIALLY) IGNORES NOT ONLY OUR
PHYSICAL BODIES BUT THAT WHOLE
EMBODIMENT WHICH CONSISTS OF OUR
FAMILY, JOB, PAST AND CONNECTIONS. AT
HOME, BESIDES BEING PETER OR JANE, WE
ALSO BEAR A GENERAL CHARACTER; HUSBAND
OR WIFE, BROTHER OR SISTER, CHIEF,
COLLEAGUE OR SUBORDINATE. NOT AMONG
OUR FRIENDS. IT IS AN AFFAIR OF
DISENTANGLED, OR STRIPPED, MINDS.
EROS WILL HAVE NAKED BODIES;
FRIENDSHIP NAKED PERSONALITIES.

C.S. LEWIS (1898-1963),
FROM *"THE FOUR LOVES: FRIENDSHIP"*

WHEN TWO PEOPLE
UNDERSTAND

*Life leads the thoughtful man on a path of
many windings.
Now the course is checked, now it runs
straight again....
But when two people are at one in their
inmost hearts,
They shatter even the strength of iron or
of bronze.
And when two people understand each other
in their inmost hearts,
Their words are sweet and strong, like the
fragrance of orchids.*

CONFUCIUS(551-479 B.C.),
FROM "FELLOWSHIP WITH MEN"

WITHOUT A FRIEND

The comfort of having a friend may be taken away, but not that of having had one.

SENECA (C.4 B.C.-A.D.65)

Robbing life of friendship is like robbing the world of the sun.

CICERO (106-43 B.C.)

When friends stop being frank and useful to each other, the whole world loses some of its radiance.

ANATOLE BROYARD (1920-1990)

No man is the whole of himself; his friends are the rest of him.

REV. HARRY EMERSON

The important people are my family and my real friends. Friends I've gone through things with. Friends who've been there in the good times (when I got married) and the bad (when we split up). Friends I've gone through pregnancy with (theirs, not mine), through broken romances, even through death. For them, I'd do anything, at any time.

TARA MCKENZIE,
FROM *"COSMOPOLITAN"*, APRIL 1995

Friends like us are undeterred by spots, fevers, overflowing washing machines, berserk spin driers, major structural repairs and Christmas holidays.
Who do we have but each other?!

PAM BROWN, b.1928

LAUGHTER

One can never speak enough of the virtues, the dangers, the power of shared laughter.

FRANCOISE SAGAN

Nobody who is afraid of laughing, and heartily too, at his friend, can be said to have a true and thorough love for him; and, on the other hand, it would portray a sorry want of faith to distrust a friend because he laughs at you. Few men, I believe, are much worth loving in whom there is not something well worth laughing at.

J.C. AND W. HARE,
FROM *"GUESSES AT TRUTH"*

THE WORDS OF FRIENDSHIP

$\mathcal{D}$id friendship between human beings come about in the first place along with – or through – the inspiration of language? It can be safe to say that when we learned to speak to, and listen to, rather than to

strike or be struck by, our fellow
human beings, we found something
worth keeping alive, worth the
possessing, for the rest of time. Might
it possibly have been the other way
round – that the promptings of
friendship guided us into learning to
express ourselves, teaching ourselves,
between us, a language to keep it by?
Friendship might have been the first,
as well as the best, teacher of
communication. Which came first,
friendship or the spoken word?
They could rise from the same
prompting: to draw together,
not to pull away, not to
threaten any longer.

EUDORA WELTY, b.1909, FROM *"THE
NORTON BOOK OF FRIENDSHIP"*

For the loftiest friendships have no commercial element in them; to the contrary, they are founded on sacrifice. They neither expect nor desire gift for gift or service for service. No bushel of friendship for a bushel of favors.

SARAH B. COOPER

Oh, my friend, is it the settled rule of life that we are to accept nothing not expensive? It is not so settled for me. That which is freest, cheapest, seems somehow more valuable than anything I pay for; that which is given, better than that which is bought; that which passes between you and me in the glance of an eye, a touch of the hand, is better than minted money!

DAVID GRAYSON (1870-1946)

KINDNESS

The best rule of friendship is to keep your heart a little softer than your head.

GEORGE SANTAYANA (1863-1952)

Have friends, not for the sake of receiving, but of giving.

JOSEPH ROUX,
FROM "MEDITATIONS OF A PARISH PRIEST"

You give but little when you give of your possessions. It is when you give of yourself that you truly give.

KAHLIL GIBRAN (1883-1931)

before

installing

officers

We are born helpless. As soon as we are fully conscious we discover loneliness. We need others physically, emotionally, intellectually. We need them if we are to know anything, even ourselves.

C.S. LEWIS (1898-1963)

Thus nature has no love for solitude, and always leans, as it were, on some support; and the sweetest support is found in the most intimate friendship.

CICERO (106-43 B.C.)

We are born helpless. As soon as we are fully conscious we discover loneliness. We need others physically, emotionally, intellectually. We need them if we are to know anything, even ourselves.

C.S. LEWIS (1898-1963)

Thus nature has no love for solitude, and always leans, as it were, on some support; and the sweetest support is found in the most intimate friendship.

CICERO (106-43 B.C.)

Under the magnetism of friendship the modest man becomes bold; the shy, confident; the lazy, active; or the impetuous, prudent and peaceful.

WILLIAM MAKEPEACE THACKERAY
(1811-1863)

Alone among unsympathetic companions, I hold certain views and standards timidly, half ashamed to avow them and half doubtful if they can after all be right. Put me back among my Friends and in half an hour – in ten minutes – these same views and standards become once more indisputable. The opinion of this little circle, while I am in it, outweighs that of a thousand outsiders:...

C.S. LEWIS (1898-1963),
FROM "THE FOUR LOVES: FRIENDSHIP"

$\mathcal{A}$ friendship counting nearly forty years
is the finest kind of shade-tree I know.

JAMES RUSSELL LOWELL

Happy to whom, in maturer season
of life, there remains one tired and
constant friend.

ANONYMOUS

It is easy to say how we love *new* friends,
and what we think of them, but words
can never trace out all the fibres that knit
us to the *old*.

GEORGE ELIOT (MARY ANN EVANS)
(1819-1880)

A day for toil, an hour for sport, but for a
friend is life too short.

RALPH WALDO EMERSON (1803-1882),
FROM *"CONSIDERATIONS BY THE WAY"*

IN A CIRCLE OF
TRUE FRIENDS

ℐN A CIRCLE OF TRUE FRIENDS EACH MAN IS SIMPLY WHAT HE IS: STANDS FOR NOTHING BUT HIMSELF. NO ONE CARES TWOPENCE ABOUT ANYONE ELSE'S FAMILY, PROFESSION, CLASS, INCOME, RACE, OR PREVIOUS HISTORY. OF COURSE YOU WILL GET TO KNOW ABOUT MOST OF THESE IN THE END. BUT CASUALLY. THEY WILL COME OUT BIT BY BIT, TO FURNISH AN ILLUSTRATION OR AN ANALOGY, TO SERVE AS PEGS FOR AN ANECDOTE; NEVER FOR THEIR OWN SAKE.

C.S. LEWIS (1898-1963),
FROM *"THE FOUR LOVES: FRIENDSHIP"*

Man is a knot, a web, a mesh into which relationships are tied. Only those relationships matter.

ANTOINE DE SAINT-EXUPERY
(1900-1944)

We cannot live only for ourselves. A thousand fibers connect us with our fellow men; and along these fibers, as sympathetic threads, our actions run as causes, and they come back as effects.

HERMAN MELVILLE (1819-1891)

There is a destiny that makes us brothers: None goes his way alone; all that we send into the lives of others comes back into our own.

EDWIN MARKHAM

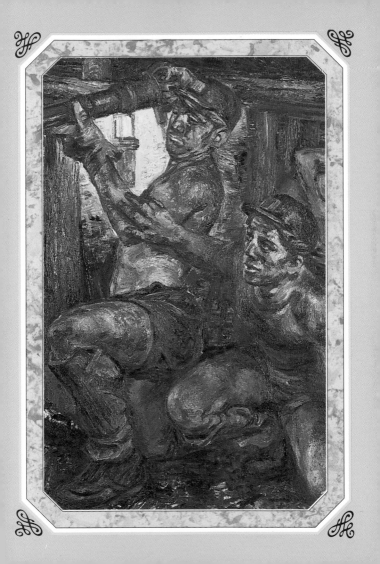

How life
catches up with
us and teaches us to
love and forgive each other.

JUDY COLLINS, b.1939

Beautiful and rich is an old friendship,
Grateful to the touch as ancient ivory,
Smooth as aged wine,
or sheen of tapestry
Where light has lingered,
intimate and long.

EUNICE TIEJENS (1884-1944)
FROM *"OLD FRIENDSHIPS"*

One needs a friend of the same age – that
way neither of you will ever notice that
you are both growing old.

PAM BROWN, b.1928

The language of friendship is not words, but meanings. It is an intelligence above language.

HENRY DAVID THOREAU (1817-1862)

… there can be no happiness equal to the joy of finding a heart that understands.

VICTOR ROBINSON

The scholar sits down to write, and all his years of meditation do not furnish him with one good thought or happy expression; but it is necessary to write a letter to a friend, – and forthwith troops of gentle thoughts invest themselves, on every hand, with chosen words.

RALPH WALDO EMERSON (1803-1882), FROM "ESSAYS: FRIENDSHIP"

To know someone here or there with whom you feel there is understanding in spite of distances or thoughts unexpressed – that can make of this earth a garden.

JOHANN WOLFGANG VON GOETHE
(1749-1832)

A SPECIAL FRIEND

Not anybody and everybody can be your friend. It must be someone as close to you as your skin, someone who imparts color, drama, meaning to your life.

HENRY MILLER (1891-1980)

… love …respect … loyalty … that, surely, is what true friendship is all about.

TARA MCKENZIE,
FROM *"COSMOPOLITAN"*, APRIL 1995

*A faithful friend is a secure shelter;
Whoever finds one has found a treasure.
A faithful friend is beyond price;
His worth is more than money can buy.
A faithful friend is an elixir of life.…*

ECCLESIASTES

WHAT WE ARE TOGETHER

We are not friends
because of the laughs
we spend
but the tears
we save.

I don't want to be near you
for the thoughts we share
but the words we never have
to speak.

I will never miss you
because of what we do
but what we are
together.

NIKKI GIOVANNI,
"A POEM OF FRIENDSHIP"